Reflections
ON
LENT

A RETICENT WANDERER'S JOURNEY

Reflections ON LENT

A RETICENT WANDERER'S JOURNEY

SHAUNA GILL

Scriptures taken from the Holy Bible, New International Version®, NIV®. Copyright © 1973, 1978, 1984, 2011 by Biblica, Inc.™ Used by permission of Zondervan. All rights reserved worldwide. www.zondervan.com The "NIV" and "New International Version" are trademarks registered in the United States Patent and Trademark Office by Biblica, Inc.™

Author photo by Expose Photography, Jacqueline Goodfellow

Soft cover ISBN: 978-1-4866-2455-3
Hard cover ISBN: 978-1-4866-2456-0
eBook ISBN: 978-1-4866-2457-7

Word Alive Press
119 De Baets Street Winnipeg, MB R2J 3R9
www.wordalivepress.ca

WORD ALIVE
—PRESS—

Cataloguing in Publication information can be obtained from Library and Archives Canada.

*This is dedicated to my mom, Sylvia Wylie.
She helped me move from Catholic to catholic.*

Acknowledgments

I would like to acknowledge the contemplative Christian faith community of SoulStream. It was Deb Arndt, the director of SoulStream, who invited me to write for our community during Lent 2023. SoulStream encourages our contemplative journey with Christ. SoulStream.org

First Week of Lent
This Little Suffering

It hasn't been my propensity to follow Lent. As a child born into the catholic faith, my early understanding of Lent was that it was a season of sadness and suffering. We took on our own little sufferings by giving up something for Lent. In this small way, we joined in the suffering of Jesus.

Oftentimes, though, because we were children, it became a competition between some of my siblings and myself. Who would fail first? Who had the strength to go the full forty days without TV, chocolate, or dessert? Could I really give my precious allowance into the offering plate at Mass each Sunday until Easter?

"Do more good," we were also encouraged. Like taking time for extra prayer, going to Mass more often, or, for us younger ones, trying to fight less with our siblings. I agreed one year to read more of my *Uncle Arthur's Bedtime Stories*, which I loved anyway. They were lovely stories about children who had faith in God and prayed. The parents in those books were always nice and kind and everything seemed quite orderly.

Once I reached adulthood, I gave up Lenten practices for years.

My first confession is that I have dismissed Lenten observances since I moved towards Protestantism some thirty-five years ago. This is exactly why I said yes to writing about Lent this year. I am grateful for the opportunity. The invitation came as a surprise, and so it felt like a true invitation.

How might I, and we, be invited to enter more deeply into Lent?

Interestingly, I gently moved back to observing Advent. I prefer the season of Advent more than Christmas itself. I find myself meditating on the idea of waiting for the one who is already here. I love this gestational idea. It seems like waiting with Mary while she grows with child. He is here but not yet. This idea helps me to remain awake and on the lookout for Christ, longing for his presence and sometimes feeling it as surely as the breeze.

Lent doesn't have quite as positive an attraction for me. Yes, that old season of sadness and suffering. Indeed,

Lent is sadder and harder and more revealing of our weak hearts.

Ah. Now there is a thread I should perhaps follow.

Finally, now, as an adult, I may have a glimmer of what it really means to give something up for Lent. It's a prompt to help me see my own weakness, to lean into how difficult it is to give up the crutches, treats, or pastimes we rely upon. In this growing awareness of my reliance on the simple pleasures of life, I can realize that perhaps, just for a time, I can say no and turn to God instead.

I easily see the sense of it now, of course. Giving up chocolate as a child might now be like giving up a five o'clock glass of wine. "Oh, I'd love a glass of wine." This thought is now a prompt for me to confess, "Lord, I lean on other things to help me through my days. My habit is to pour this wine, to temporarily feel less stress, and perhaps ignore, even for a short time, the little sufferings in my life. I long to numb the memories, the loneliness, the sense of emptiness that seems to come at this witching hour. Lord, I give this up, trusting that you will be with me in the loneliness. In your love, help me to trust that I need not cover up or hide my pain."

That's hard.

This little suffering is a prompt for self-examination, prayer, hope, and fostering a willingness to be transformed by fully repenting of whatever it is we rely upon more than God. We let go of one thing and open ourselves to being filled with something else, something far more beautiful and sustaining: the Holy Spirit.

I understand this now. Already this year Lent has brought me closer to the sense of God with me—that Advent descriptor, Emmanuel. God with us, here also in Lent.

Amen.

Questions to Ponder

1. Are there things upon which you lean on for support or depend on to numb pain in your life?

2. When you consider these things, what feelings arise?

3. Consider God loving you in this moment. What can help with this? Perhaps some silence, the lighting of a candle, or taking a slow walk.

4. Take some time to be with God.

Second Week of Lent
If We Fail? No, When We Fail

In this second week of Lent, I have mulled over the words I wrote last week about being a sibling and wondering who among us would fail first at whatever we were giving up for Lent. Oh, that integral competitive nature of humans!

I'm drawn to consider this idea a little further, but hopefully with more grace than merely asking, "Who will fail first?" In Lent, we can set out to give something up and instead turn to be with God. What do we do with our failures? What does Jesus do with our failures?

In my imagination, I join the disciples in the garden of Gethsemane with Jesus (Matthew 26:38–46, Mark 14:37–40, Luke 22:40–46, John 18). Jesus wants his friends to stay awake and be present with him while he prays. He wants them to pray as well, to take an active role while they wait for him.

The disciples can't do it. Jesus is in emotional agony. His soul is *"overwhelmed with sorrow to the point of death"* (Matthew 26:38). As well, *"being in anguish, he prayed more earnestly, and his sweat was like drops of blood falling to the ground"* (Luke 22:44).

Just a few meters away from him, the disciples are snoozing.

When he goes back to his disciples, what I hear in Jesus is disappointment: *"Couldn't you men keep watch with me for one hour?"* (Matthew 26:40)

Their eyes are heavy.

"The spirit is willing, but the flesh is weak," says Jesus (Matthew 26:41).

Only in Luke do we read further of the disciples' emotional condition. They were exhausted from sorrow.

Falling asleep, as Luke implies, can be a coping mechanism. This makes me think of those who suffer deep depression. They can't get out of bed. They sleep because they feel unable to cope with the weight of their feelings and their perception of the enormity and seeming hopelessness of life.

So Jesus's closest friends and followers have let him down. As one of his followers, how do I take that in? Personally, of course, I'd rather not fail. To fail Jesus so deeply and scandalously in his hour of need seems impossible!

Perhaps this is also part of my unwillingness to enter the season of Lent for so many years. What if it's too hard to stay awake? What if I fail at what I set out to do? What if my spirit isn't willing? Really. Sometimes it's not.

It's way easier not to bother. Instead of going to the garden with Jesus, maybe I would have stayed back to do the dishes after the Passover meal. I might protect myself completely from the possibility of failure.

There it is. My ego protecting itself. My ego never seems to want to be human, although it sure is good at protecting its tender human soul.

What did Jesus do with the disciples' failure and his own disappointment? He doesn't shame them for their human response. He doesn't shame himself for his human fear, doubt, anxiety, or tears. Jesus doesn't say, "Father, I'm sorry I'm scared. I'm sorry, but I'd rather not do this." Instead he just leans into his humanity and lets it be what it is.

Nor does Jesus apologize for his disappointment. He lets his own disappointment be. It is a matter of fact. It is. He knows that humanity is frail, and he is too. It's so easy for me to forget this. He is fully God and fully human. We get tired. We get afraid. We are disappointing and we get disappointed. We get sad and want to check out. We'd rather go to bed.

Jesus doesn't spend time belabouring the point that he is disappointed. There are other things to move on to. More important things. And interestingly, his disappointment and their abandonment are all part of the gig. Jesus doesn't focus on their abandonment, but rather on what God has for him to do.

How interesting it is for us to think of the people who have disappointed or abandoned us. We can consider whether this is part of the gig for us too. Why would we be exempt?

Can I, like Jesus, let go of the disappointments? Can I forgive and get on with the next thing God has for me? Can I let go of the self-abasement that always comes for me when I've disappointed another? I'm not suggesting that I bury these human frailties, but rather that I acknowledge them, look at them, and then offer them back to the God who made me. Through this, I take an active role in embracing and forgiving my frailty, such that I can move on, try again, and start fresh rather than wallow.

First, can I continue to give up my patterns of shame and self-recrimination this Lent? Can I deeply believe that when God saw what he created in humanity, it was very good? Can I stop apologizing for my humanity? Can I remember that Jesus did not apologize for his humanity?

Second, can I give up the idea that a person's disappointment in me or something I've done doesn't mean they don't love me? Can I give up my deep fear of disappointment?

I will disappoint, and I will be disappointed. It just is. Jesus accepts his disappointment, but he doesn't belabour it. He keeps moving forward, knowing that a little bruise on his heart is the least of his worries.

Lord, this Lent help me to appreciate on a new level your acceptance of your humanity. May your life in me encourage me to accept my own humanity without shame a little more each day. Help me to trust that love can overcome even our deepest disappointment.

Amen.

Questions to Ponder

1. In which ways have you coped with disappointment and failure?

2. Is there a way in which you coped with disappointment or failure that you feel needs forgiveness?

3. Is it possible for you to forgive yourself if you aren't happy with how you coped?

4. Are there others you can ask forgiveness from?

5. Consider how Jesus's humanity might help you accept your own humanity.

6. Take some time to be with God.

Third Week of Lent

Lean Ever Nearer To

I woke up early one day last week with the word Lent on my mind. In the moments between sleep and waking up, I felt a new invitation. I thought of the letters and how they might form an acrostic poem to simplify some of what I have been longing to understand about Lent.

This seems to be an answer to the prayer of my heart. Lord, what does Lent mean for me?

I skimmed over this liturgical season throughout the years because of its seeming religiosity. Lent culminates in Holy Week, which includes the passion narratives. The symbols and solemnity of this time in the Catholic church of my youth are shrouded in uncomfortable memories.

My questions weren't handled with grace, so I left the season behind for decades.

So, on this morning, in the gentle moments before fully awakening, I heard the whisper of the Holy Spirit in my heart:

Lean
Ever
Nearer
To

Wow. That sounded gentle.

This allowed my imagination to flow freely with what I had been learning and pondering so far this season of Lent. It opened the heart of my eighteen-year-old self who didn't want to enter spiritual activities she didn't feel sincere about. It opened my heart to say, "Yes, I can do this. I can lean into things with curiosity, and wonder, and even uncertainty now, because it doesn't feel threatening."

As I consider what I might be able to lean ever nearer to, within this context of Lent, I find myself thinking of so many possibilities:

- I lean into the story of Jesus in the desert.
- I lean into what tempts me and where my own weaknesses lie.
- I lean into honesty.
- I lean into the truth of my humanity, which isn't for shame to grow but rather for compassion to grow, both for myself and others.

- I lean into the idea that Jesus came to show us the spiritual rhythm of our lives. He suffered all the human horror in his short life, leaving us open to the truth that he understands our sorrows. He gets how it feels to be misunderstood, denied, abandoned, mocked, and bullied. He knows what it feels like to be murdered. He as God understands, and we are never alone.
- And finally, perhaps I can lean into a greater openness towards the idea that the season of Lent may surprise me in its ability to transform my religiously closed heart.

Lean ever nearer to… Perhaps you sense your own invitation to lean into Lent in some way this season.

Amen.

Questions to Ponder

1. How do the words "lean ever nearer to" resonate with you? Do you sense an invitation from God for you to lean ever nearer to something specific this Lent?

2. Are there some things you'd like to lean nearer to within yourself?

3. Do you feel invited to lean nearer to certain things with God?

4. Take some time to be with God.

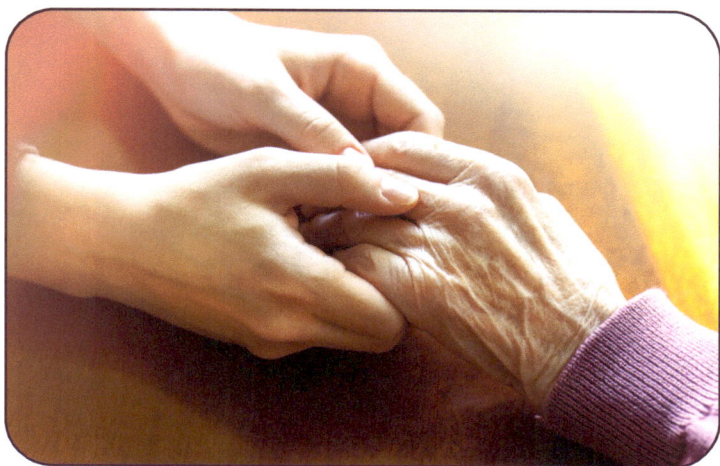

As I continue to recall the Lenten practices I experienced in my youth, and consider Lent this year, I will now lean ever nearer towards my mom's encouragement: "Do more good." I like the simplicity of this.

Here's what I found online:

> Throughout our history, Christians have found prayer, fasting, and almsgiving to be an important part of repentance and renewal. Many Catholics now add something during Lent rather than giving up something, either to address personal habits

that need work or to add some outreach to others in need…

A good practice is to do something extra in prayer, something involving fasting (whether limiting our intake of food or giving up something non food-related), and something involving almsgiving (giving money or goods to the needy or doing extra acts of charity).[1]

I like this choice. I personally feel more drawn to offering acts of charity than giving something up. To be honest, I think it feels easier for my personality type.

For years, being a registered nurse and a mother felt as easy to me as breathing. I offered compassion, gentleness, and even humour freely and effortlessly.

However, there are hazards. How do I watch out for the ego trap? How do I listen well to the motive of my heart? Is it even possible to have pure motives? Maybe that's also part of the process of embracing my humanity.

Three specific contemplations help me discern whether I am to do something. They guide me when I want to offer some aspect of who I am or what I have during Lent.

The first prayer contains questions. Am I drawn to do this thing? I tend to look for how gentle something feels, how invitational. In considering it, I listen for the Holy Spirit. Alternatively, do I feel more driven to do this? Perhaps I feel competitive. I feel like I "should" do it, or even

---

[1] "Lent in the Catholic Church," *About Catholics*. Date of access: December 7, 2023 (https://www.aboutcatholics.com/beliefs/lent-in-the-catholic-church).

a degree of guilt if I don't. These sneaky mindsets can motivate me to move forward with caution.

A second prayer causes me to ask, "What is mine to do?" This simple guiding prayer has been hard won. My charitable personality can get me into trouble. This prayer has grown in soil formed by years of giving myself away, pleasing others, and sometimes working very hard to make changes when the proper time for that change had not yet come.

And finally, I live by a simple mantra from Mother Teresa: "There are no great things, only small things with great love."[2] These words have helped me slow down and do even the simplest of things with a more sensitive motive. Making sandwiches for my husband and I to have for lunch can be a spiritual offering when done with care and attention.

Currently, I'm on winter vacation. Considering Lent feels like my prayerful sacrifice for this time. I have committed a part of my heart and mind to leaning into what this season might teach me and share my ponderings. When I was invited to undertake this project, I felt drawn to it.

I often find myself here on my vacation, considering Lent and my thoughts and feelings about it. What am I to share, God? What am I drawn to about Lent? What is rising within me? It's a good and gentle practice to peck away, to trust that everything shall emerge as it is supposed

---

to as I move from lounging by the pool back to the casa to jot down some more thoughts.

Is this enough to be called a Lenten sacrifice? I'll trust it is.

Amen.

Questions to Ponder

1. How do you make decisions pertaining to what you offer the world?

2. Many people get caught up in giving too much of themselves. Fatigue and even burnout can set in. What helps you to make decisions around setting boundaries for yourself?

3. Consider some of the things that motivate you to do, or not do, "more good."

4. Take some time to be with God.

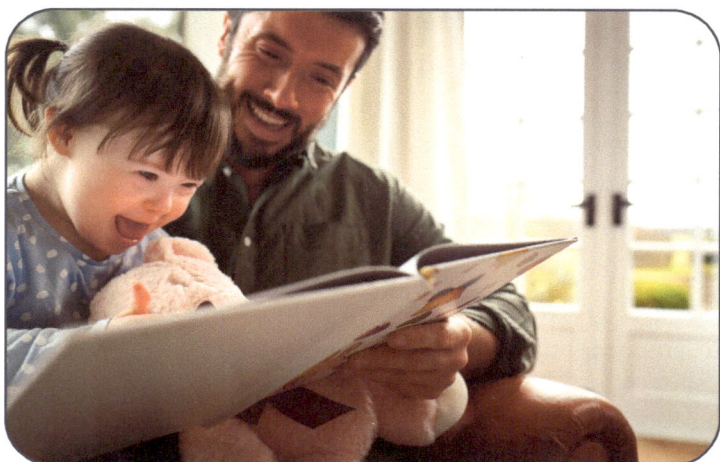

Fifth Week of Lent
Leaning into Change

One of the underlying truths in life is that change is inevitable. We start in the womb, and in order for us to move forward into life we must be birthed.

This dramatic first release ends with the severing of the umbilical cord. With that cut, the infant's blood supply changes; it is no longer a shared supply with the mother. With her first breath, the child's tiny heart must accommodate this physical change. It begins pumping the blood still remaining in her system. A portion of the mother's blood becomes her own.

With the cutting of this cord, the child is released into her own separate life. She has been born.

Though there are no nerve endings in the umbilical cord, the wound still needs time to heal. Conscientious and tender care is needed and we are all left with a scar.

Consider all the changes and losses you have gone through in your life. Consider the planned changes, and the ones you have little to no control over. We experience some of these changes gradually as we age. Others are sudden and shocking. The intense pain of having something severed from us is a common human experience. It doesn't always make as much logical sense as with the newborn. It can be confusing and deeply unsettling.

Loss and grief are deeply personal, and our personalities impact how much we suffer. Have you ever had to move away from your best friend? Have you ever experienced the sudden death of someone you loved deeply? In both cases, the severing can feel like a physical death. The grief can be paralyzing. We need time to process, grieve, and find a new way forward. The cut cord within our heart needs tender care in order for us to heal.

Consider how the disciples must have felt as Jesus started to leave hints that the end of their time together was drawing near. They didn't want to believe it. There was so much they didn't understand.

Even when we know we're going to lose something, we don't want to believe it. We can't imagine what life might be like until we're faced with the everydayness of living without an important person, a capability we used to have, a job we loved, a home, or a church we once belonged to.

Jesus felt severed from his Father as he hung on the cross: *"My God, my God, why have you forsaken me?"* (Matthew 27:46, Mark 15:34)

I've often marvelled at people who experience a great loss and feel deeply changed for the better. They may say, for example, "I can't imagine my life without this special needs child. We love her so much. She has opened our hearts to unconditional love." My own experience would have me say, "I am so grateful for how God met me in my own deep loss and grief. I now have a deeper and more authentic relationship with God."

Herein lies the renewal. This is new life. We are born again.

Have you ever felt severed from something very important to you? Paying attention to ourselves can help us respond to changes and losses. It's possible for some of us to hang on to being "fine" and stubbornly refuse the vulnerability that healing requires. We may be very angry, depressed, or bitter. These emotions can inhibit grief from softening our hearts.

These very human ways of coping with pain can make it difficult for new life to sprout in our hearts. As a spiritual director, I accompany people on the journey of opening their hearts to the healing God can offer us. The process can be excruciatingly slow. The time it takes is the time it takes.

According to Luke, Jesus's final words spoke of trust after all he'd been through: *"Father, into your hands I commit my spirit"* (Luke 23:46).

May we be awake enough in our own changes and losses to trust in the process of time. May we open ourselves to whatever newness God has for us in the regeneration of our spirits. May we be born again.

Amen.

Questions to Ponder

1. Consider some of the losses you have faced in your life.

2. In what ways have you coped well with loss?

3. Are there some coping mechanisms that haven't been helpful for you?

4. In what ways have you experienced new life after a loss?

5. Take some time to be with God.

Sixth Week of Lent
Forgiveness of Sins

My heart is not proud, Lord, my eyes are not haughty; I do not concern myself with great matters or things too wonderful for me. But I have calmed and quieted myself, I am like a weaned child with its mother; like a weaned child I am content. Israel, put your hope in the Lord both now and forevermore. (Psalm 131:1–3)

Looking up at the life-sized crucifix in the Catholic church as a child was frightening. The idea that I had some responsibility in putting Jesus there scared the heck out of me. For years, this sealed my image of God as a judging, disappointed Father.

Later, as I became a born-again Christian, I believed that only those of us who intellectually and heartfully accept Jesus into our hearts are saved. Professing faith that he died for my personal sins became my ticket to heaven.

A complete deconstruction of my life from 2004 to 2007 was transformative for me. A litany of losses shook everything in which I believed. In those years, God's loving Spirit touched me to my core.

Now I'm less worried about doctrine and more awake to listening to the truth of God in my heart. First comes contemplation, then action, followed by more contemplation. Waiting. Discerning. Listening.

In the years since this deconstruction, I have been consoled by Psalm 131 as I lean into the things of God with less intellectual certainty. Jesus's words allow me to be open to the truth: I also have no idea. *"Father, forgive them, for they do not know what they are doing"* (Luke 23:34). What sins have I committed that I'm not awake to? Who have I hurt? Sometimes I know, but other times I may not.

Why wouldn't I know?

I am hard on myself by nature. It's easier for me to feel compassion for myself and others when I add context to the word *sin*. Words like *woundedness*, *brokenness*, and *weakness* help me. We all have the human propensity to fall short of the glory of God, and these more expansive words open my heart to welcoming, understanding, and compassion. They open my heart to our shared sorrow.

Trying to figure it all out doctrinally can feel too grand for me. Too wondrous. I hope this doesn't sound like a copout, but rather a long struggled-for state of rest.

Someone once, and perhaps incorrectly, described the weaned child in Psalm 131 as one who is finished his feeding. He just pulls off his mother's breast and falls asleep in her arms. That image has stuck with me for years. As we continue to grow spiritually, perhaps our need for certainty in doctrine gently falls away.

As I've considered the last week of Lent and Jesus's final days, my attention has been drawn to the cast of characters in the story. Judas. Peter. The other disciples asking whether they'll deny Jesus. Pilot. Caiaphas. The Roman soldiers.

I wonder... given the pressures of power, politics, culture, economics, personality, and expectations, where would I be in this story? We often think, "Oh, I would never do that." As humans, though, one of our first words seems to be "Baaaa." We follow like sheep to the slaughter.

Consider how many people went along with the savagery of the slave trade, the atrocities of Nazi Germany, or the Rwandan genocide of 1994. We keep ourselves willfully blind to the profits of pharmaceutical companies.

No, I haven't been drawn into anything as tragic as that.

However, at times I have been the metaphorically crucified. At other times I have been the crucifier. I am the betrayed and the betrayer. I am the abandoned and the one who abandons. I am denied and I am the one who denies. Thinking anything else just isn't true.

Jesus doesn't judge anyone, not even his murderers. He accepts the brokenness of humanity. He forgives their brutality. He forgives their deep misunderstanding over who he was and his mission. Even for his closest friends, he prayed, *"Father, forgive them…"*

"Follow me," Jesus says to us. "Do what I do. Forgive. Be a healing presence in the world. Hold open your hands in trust of my Father, who knows all and redeems all."

This is a mystery too marvellous for me to figure out. For me today, holding to a line of doctrine seems to rob these words of their tenderness. In the period of Eastertide after this period of Lent, dwell on this wondrous love, this wondrous comfort!

May we rest in this wonder.

Amen.

Questions to Ponder

1. Extending forgiveness can be life-changing. What is one thing you would like to forgive yourself for?

2. Sometimes it's very difficult to forgive ourselves and others. Does it feel possible to accept that broken part of yourself? Does it feel possible to you, in the presence of our loving God, to forgive that inability to forgive?

3. Is there something within you, or in someone else, that you feel you have fully forgiven?

4. Can you sense its healing within your heart?

5. I encourage you to smile about this full or even partial forgiveness.

6. Take some time with God.

About the Author

Shauna Gill has been a trauma nurse, a nurse educator and a parish nurse. She has her Master of Nursing and holds certificates in Parish Nursing, Spiritual Direction, and Spiritual Formation. Shauna has experience in retreat care and leading contemplative experiences for groups. She has three adult offspring, and lives with her husband Dave in British Columbia's Okanagan Valley. There, she is inspired by the outdoors as well as the joy and pain of living an ever more contemplative life in Christ.

Shauna has published a children's book through Word Alive Press, *Henrick the Rooster Learns to Be Kind.* She is currently working on a memoir through Tall Pine Press.

Also by Shauna Gill

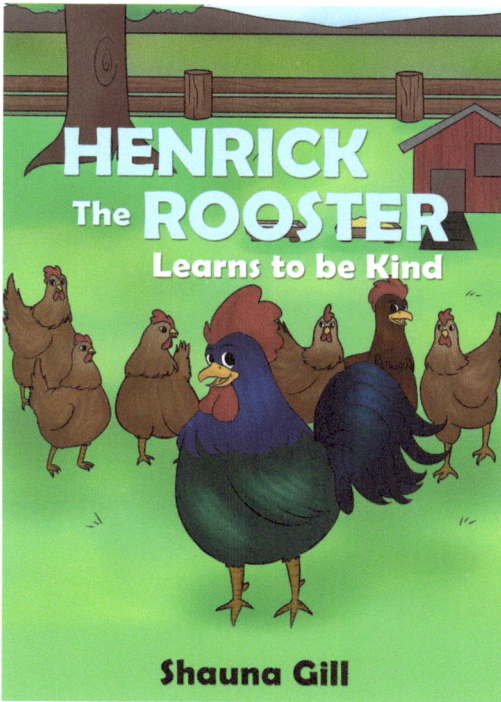

Henrick the Rooster Learns to be Kind

Henrick is a beautiful, young rooster who has some important lessons to learn about kindness, friendship, and being humble. Through Henrick, children will learn about the natural behaviours of roosters, and that there is more to growing up than just becoming big and strong. Henrick goes on an emotional journey to learn how to be a mature rooster.

www.ingramcontent.com/pod-product-compliance
Lightning Source LLC
Chambersburg PA
CBHW041819040426
42452CB00004B/150